Prayers for Guidance

Tara Caputo

Dedication

    I dedicate this book to my mom. She is the angel on my shoulder who always guides, protects and opens my doors. No matter where I go I will always carry you in my heart.

    I also dedicate this book to my husband Anthony and our adorable little angel Anthony, Jr. Without the two of you I don't know where I would be today. You two give me the strength to always keep moving forward. What I do is always for the two of you. Love you to pieces.

    To my dad, you are the strongest individual I ever met. I wouldn't be the person I am today without you. To my brother Paul, sorry I always sound like a mom, but hey that's what sisters are for. No matter what I am always here for the both of you.

INTRODUCTION

The contents of this book are to help and guide you in your times of need and it could also be used with your daily rituals. Everyone's beliefs are different that's why I have combined religious prayers with spiritual prayers. For those of you who know me, know I am a very spiritual person but I am also very big with angels and saints. I believe if you put all your energy, focus and believe your prayers will be answered.

Prayers are extremely powerful when you put your full energy and belief into them. Not everything happens right away but in time and with a little bit of faith it will. So I have decided to share my prayers that I use in my times in the need with you. Keep in mind it does not contain all the Saints. In Prayers for Guidance you will find powerful Novena's, Psalms, prayers and spiritual prayers. I also listed the candle color and the day of the week to light the candle for your intention.

I hope this book helps you with all your needs and intentions.

Many Blessings to all.

PRAYER INDEX

1. *Prayer for Health........................pg14*
2. *Prayer for Special Intentions.....pg 14,20, 22, 23*
3. *Prayer for Protection.........pg 8,14 16,,25,28*
4. *Prayer to become pregnant.....pg13,18*
5. *Prayer for court cases..............pg 5,22*
6. *Prayer for Communication........pg 5*
7. *Prayer for Peace........................pg29,41*
8. *Prayer for Healing....................pg 6,19,34*
9. *Prayer In Time of Need...............pg13,22*
10. *Prayer for Job............................pg16*
11. *Prayer for Home ....pg 8,16*
12. *Prayer for Blessing in the Home......pg12,16*
13. *Prayer to fight evil............................pg8,25,28*
14. *Prayer for Married Couples............pg 16*
15. *Prayer for Love.................................pg 6,20*
16. *Prayer for Mothers..............pg 13, 18,23*
17. *Prayer for Mediumship........pg18, 26,28*
18. *Prayer for Safe Trip...................pg6*
19. *Prayer for Special Request......................pg 14,18,20,22*
20. *Prayer for Financial Problems....pg20,32*
21. *Prayer for Lost Articles..............pg20*
22. *Prayer for Substance Abuse...........pg 28*
23. *Prayer to Restore Faith....................pg28*
24. *Prayer for Money............ ....pg32*
25. *Prayer for Messages............................pg5*
26. *Prayer for Reunited w/Loved Ones..............pg 6*
27. *Prayer to Open Roads..............pg33*
28. *Prayer to Conquer Enemies...........pg 8*
29. *For Happiness........................pg 12, 28,23*
30. *Special Novenas.................pg 14,36,38, 39,39,43*

Archangel/St. Gabriel

Saint Gabriel the Archangel, I venerate you as the Angel of the Incarnation, because God specially appointed you to bear the messages concerning the God-Man to Daniel, Zechariah, and the Blessed Virgin Mary. Give me a very tender and devoted love for the Incarnate Word and his Blessed Mother more like your own. I venerate you also as the "Strength from God" because you are the giver of God's strength, consoler and comforter chosen to strengthen God's faithful and teach them important truths. I ask for the grace of a special power of the will to strive for holiness of life.

Steady my resolutions; renew my courage; comfort and console me in the problems, trials and sufferings of daily living, as you consoled our Savior in his agony and Mary in her sorrows and Joseph in his trials. I put my confidence in you. Saint Gabriel I ask you especially for this favor: *(mention your request)*. Through your earnest love for the Son of God made man and for his Blessed Mother I beg of you, intercede for me that my request may be granted, if it be God's holy will. Pray for us, Saint Gabriel the Archangel, that we may be worthy of the promises of Christ. Amen.

Patron Saint: Saint Gabriel is the patron saint of messengers, communication workers, and postal workers

Archangel/St. Raphael

Feast Day: *September 29*
Candle Color*: Pink*

Prayer for Healing

Glorious Archangel St. Raphael, great prince of the heavenly court, you are illustrious for your gifts of wisdom and grace. You are a guide of those who journey by land or sea or air, consoler of the afflicted, and refuge of sinners.

I beg you, assist me in all my needs and in all the sufferings of this life, as once you helped the young Tobias on his travels. Because you are the "medicine of God" I humbly pray you to heal the many infirmities of my soul and the ills that afflict my body. I especially ask of you the favor (here mention your special intention), and the great grace of purity to prepare me to be the temple of the Holy Spirit. Amen.

Prayer Before a Trip

Dear St. Raphael, your lovely name means "God heals." The Lord sent you to young Tobias to guide him throughout a long journey. Upon his return you taught him how to cure his father's blindness. How natural, therefore, for Christians to pray for your powerful help for safe travel and a happy return. This is what we ask for ourselves as well as for all who are far from home. Amen.

Patron Saint for: Lovers, nurses, physicians, druggist, eye disease

Petition: Cure of sickness, safe travel, to be reunited with loved ones, in times of need, to keep away evil spirits

Archangel/St. Michael

Feast Day: *September 29th*
Candle Color: *Red, Purple and Green*

ORIGINAL ST. MICHAEL PRAYER

O Most Glorious Prince of the Heavenly Armies, St. Michael the Archangel, defend us in the battle and in our wrestling against principalities and powers, against the rulers of the world of this darkness, against the spirits of wickedness in the high places (Eph 6:12). Come to the aid of men, whom GOD created incorruptible, and to the Image of His own Likeness He made him (Wis 2:23); and from the tyranny of the devil He bought him at a great price (Cor 7:23).

Fight the battles of the Lord today with the Army of the Blessed Angels, as once thou did fight against Lucifer, the leader of pride, and his apostate angels; and they prevailed not: neither was their place found anymore in Heaven. But that great dragon was cast out, the old serpent, who is called the Devil and Satan, who seduces the whole world. And he was cast unto the earth, and his angels were thrown down with him (Rv 12:8-9).

Behold, the ancient enemy and murderer strongly raises his head! Transformed into an angel of light, with the entire horde of wicked spirits he goes about everywhere and takes possession of the earth, so that therein he may blot out the Name of GOD and of His Christ; and steal away, afflict, and ruin into everlasting destruction, the souls destined for a Crown of Eternal Glory. On men depraved in mind and corrupt in heart the wicked dragon pours out, like a most foul river, the poison of his villany; a spirit of lying, impiety and blasphemy; and the deadly breath of lust, and of all iniquities and vices. Her most crafty enemies have engulfed the Church, the Spouse of the Immaculate Lamb, with sorrows, they have drenched her with wormwood; on all her desirable things they have laid their wicked hands.

Where the See of the Blessed Peter and the Chair of Truth have been set up for the light of the world, there they have placed the throne of the abomination of their wickedness, so that, the Pastor having been struck, they may also be able to scatter the flock. Therefore, O thou unconquerable Leader, be present with the people of GOD and against the spiritual wickedness which are bursting in upon them; and bring them the victory.

The Holy Church venerates thee as its Guardian and Patron; and it glories in the fact that thou art its Defender against the wicked powers of earth and Hell. To thee the Lord has assigned the souls of the redeemed, to be placed in Heavenly bliss. Beseech the GOD of Peace to crush Satan under our feet, that he may no more be able to hold men captive and to harm the Church. Offer our prayers in the sight of the Most High, so that the mercies of the Lord may quickly come to our aid, that thou may seize the dragon, the ancient serpent, who is the Devil and Satan and that having bound him, thou may cast him into the bottomless pit, so that he may no more seduce the nations (Rv 20:3).

L. Behold the Cross of the Lord, flee away ye hostile forces. R. *The lion of the tribe of Juda, the root of David, hath conquered.*

L. May Thy mercy, O Lord, be upon us. R. *Since we have hoped in Thee.*

L. O Lord, hear my prayer. R. *And let my cry come unto Thee.*

LET US PRAY:

O GOD and Father of Our Lord Jesus Christ, we invoke Thy Holy Name, and we humbly implore Thy mercy, that by the intercession of the Mother of GOD, Mary, Immaculate Ever Virgin, of Blessed Michael the Archangel, of Blessed Joseph the Spouse of the same Blessed Virgin, of the Blessed Apostles Peter and Paul and of all the Saints, Thou wouldst deign to afford us help against Satan and all the other unclean spirits, and against whatever wanders throughout the world, to do harm to the human race and to ruin souls, through the same Christ Our Lord. Amen.

Short Version

St. Michael the Archangel, defend us in battle. Be our defense against the wickedness and snares of the Devil. May God rebuke him, we humbly pray, and do thou, O Prince of the heavenly hosts, by the power of God, thrust into hell Satan, and all the evil spirits, who prowl about the world seeking the ruin of souls. Amen.

Patron Saint of: Police Officers, Firefighters and radiologists

Petition for protection of enemies, evil and harm, victory at battle, for protection of the home and/or business

GUARDIAN ANGEL PRAYER

Angel of God, my guardian dear, to whom His love entrusts me here, ever this day [night] be at my side to light and guard, to rule and guide. Amen.

PRAYER TO MY GURADIAN ANGEL

Angel of God's light, whom God sends as a companion for me on earth, protect me from the snares of the devil, and help me to walk always as a child of God, my Creator.
Angel of God's truth, whose perfect knowledge serves what is true, protect me from deceits and temptations. Help me to know the truth, and always to live the truth.
Angel of God's love, who praises Jesus Christ, the only Son of God, who sacrificed His life for love of us, sustain me as I learn the ways of Divine love, of sacrificial generosity, of meekness and lowliness of heart.
Thank You, my heavenly friend, for your watchfull care. At the moment of my death, bring me to heaven, where the one true God, Who is light, Truth and Love, lives and reigns forever and ever.
Amen.

DAY OF THE WEEK: MONDAY
CANDLE COLOR: WHITE

BLESSED MOTHER

Hail Holy Queen

Hail, holy Queen, Mother of Mercy, Our life, our sweetness and our hope. To thee do we cry, poor banished children of Eve, To thee do we send up our sighs, Mourning and weeping in this valley of tears. Turn then, most gracious Advocate, thine eyes of mercy toward us, And after this our exile, show unto us the blessed fruit of thy womb, Jesus. O clement, O loving, O sweet Virgin Mary! Pray for us, O Holy Mother of God, That we may be made worthy of the promises of Christ. Amen.

Hail Mary

Hail Mary, full of grace, the Lord is with thee; blessed are thou among women, and blessed is the fruit of thy womb, Jesus. Holy Mary, Mother of God, pray for us sinners, now and at the hour of our death. Amen.

Mary, Help of Those in Need

Holy Mary, help those in need, give strength to the weak, comfort the sorrowful, pray for God's people, assist the clergy, intercede for religious. Mary all who seek your help experience your unfailing protection. Amen.

Infant Jesus of Prague

Feast Day: December 25th
Day of the Week: Monday
Candle Color: Orange or Red

O Jesus, Who has said, "Ask and you shall receive, seek and you shall find, knock and it shall be opened," through the intercession of Mary, Your Most Holy Mother, I knock, I seek, I ask that my prayer be granted.

(Make your request)

O Jesus, Who has said, "All that you ask of the Father in My Name, He will grant you," through the intercession of Mary Your Most Holy Mother, I humbly and urgently ask your Father in your name that my prayer will be granted.

(Make your request)

O Jesus, Who has said, "Heaven and earth shall pass away but My word shall not pass away," through the intercession of Mary Your Most Holy Mother, I feel confident that my prayer will be granted.

(Make your request)

Used in matters of health, surgeries, special requests and guidance.

This is a very powerful novena and can be used for any reason necessary.

St. Joseph

Feast Day: March 19th
Day of the Week: Sunday
Candle Color: Yellow

Oh, St. Joseph, whose protection is so great, so strong, so prompt before the throne of God. I place in you all my interests and desires. Oh, St. Joseph, do assist me by your powerful intercession, and obtain for me from your divine Son all spiritual blessings, through Jesus Christ, our Lord. So that, having engaged here below your heavenly power, I may offer my thanksgiving and homage to the most loving of Fathers.

Oh, St. Joseph, I never weary of contemplating you, and Jesus asleep in your arms; I dare not approach while He reposes near your heart. Press Him in my name and kiss His fine head for me and ask him to return the Kiss when I draw my dying breath. St. Joseph, Patron of departing souls - Pray for me.

This prayer was found in the fifteenth year of Our Lord and Savior Jesus Christ. In 1505 it was sent from the Pope to Emperor Charles when he was going into battle. Whoever shall read this prayer or hear it or keep it about themselves, shall never die a sudden death, or be drowned, not shall poison take effect of them; neither shall they fall into the hands of the enemy; or shall be burned in any fire, or shall be overpowered in battle.

Say for nine mornings for anything you may desire. It has never been known to fail, so be sure you really want what you ask.

Patron Saint of Carpenters

Petition for: protection, to find job or home, in cases of doubt and hesitation and for married couples

St. Gerard

Feast Day: October 16th
Day of the Week: Monday
Candle Color: White

A Prayer to St. Gerard for Motherhood

O glorious Saint Gerard, powerful intercessor before God, and wonder worker of our day, I call upon you and seek your help. You who always fulfilled God's will on earth, help me to do God's holy will. Intercede with the Giver of life, from whom all parenthood proceeds, that I may conceive and raise children who will please God in this life, and be heirs to the kingdom of heaven. Amen.

For Special Blessings

Dear Saint Gerard we rejoice in thy happiness and glory; we bless the Lord Who endowed thee with the choicest gifts of His Grace; we congratulate thee for corresponding so faithfully with them. Obtain for us, we pray thee, some part of thy angelic purity, thy burning love for Jesus in the Tabernacle, thy tender devotion to Mary Immaculate. In thy brotherly love which made thee the support of the poor, the comforter of the afflicted and the apostle of the most forsaken souls, grant me the favors for which I now pray.

(Here mention them privately)O most Powerful Patron, who hast always helped those who prayed to thee intercede for me before the Throne of God. O Good Saint, to thee I confide my fervent prayers; graciously accept them and, before the end of these days of prayer, let me experience in some way the effects of thy powerful intercession. Amen.

For a Sick Person

O God, Who didst bestow on Saint Gerard the power of healing all kinds of infirmities, deign to glorify Thy Servant, who was so merciful toward human misery, by delivering me from my present sickness. Grant also that, being strengthened in body, I may take greater care to avoid sin and overcome my evil passions, the spiritual diseases that drag so many to everlasting death. Through Christ our Lord. Amen.

Patron Saint of expectant mothers

Petition for: mothers with small children, to become pregnant, channeling, mediumship, expectant mothers, healing and truth.

St. Anthony

Feast Day: June 13th
Day of the Week: Tuesday
Candle Color: Brown, Orange and Green

This prayer to St. Anthony asks for help in finding missing items:

Saint Anthony, perfect imitator of Jesus, who received from God the special power of restoring lost things, grant that I may find (mention your petition) which has been lost. As least restore to me peace and tranquility of mind, the loss of which has afflicted me even more than my material loss.

To this favor I ask another of you: that I may always remain in possession of the true good that is God. Let me rather lose all things than lose God, my supreme good. Let me never suffer the loss of my greatest treasure, eternal life with God. Amen.

Prayer to Saint Anthony

Wondrous Saint Anthony, glorious for the fame of your miracles, you had the happiness of receiving in your arms our blessed Lord as a little child. Obtain for me from His mercy this favor that I desire from the bottom of my heart: (mention your request)

Since you were so gracious to poor sinners, do not regard the lack of merit on the part of him who calls upon you, but consider the glory of God, which will by exalted once more through you, by the salvation of my soul and the granting of the petition that I now earnestly present to you.

As a pledge of my gratitude, I beg you to accept my promise to live henceforth more faithfully according to the teaching of the Gospel and to be devoted to the service of the poor whom you ever loved and still love so much. Bless this my resolution and obtain for me the grace to be faithful to it till death. Amen.

Patron Saint of: lost articles and said to be a wonder worker

Petition for: special request, lost articles, for marriage or love problems and to overcome financial problems.

St. Jude

Feast Day: October 28th
Day of the Week: Sunday
Candle Color: Green, White, Red

O most holy apostle, Saint Jude, faithful servant and friend of Jesus, the Church honoureth and invoketh thee universally, as the patron of hopeless cases, and of things almost despaired of.

Pray for me, who am so miserable. Make use, I implore thee, of that particular privilege accorded to thee, to bring visible and speedy help where help was almost despaired of.

Come to mine assistance in this great need, that I may receive the consolation and succor of Heaven in all my necessities, tribulations, and sufferings, particularly (here make your request) and that I may praise God with thee and all the elect throughout eternity.

I promise thee, O blessed Jude, to be ever mindful of this great favour, to always honour thee as my special and powerful

patron, and to gratefully encourage devotion to thee.

Amen.

Petition for: hopeless cases, special request

St. Anne

Feast Day: July 26th
Day of the Week: Monday
Candle Color: White

St Anne Prayer (To Obtain Some Special Favor)

Glorious St. Ann, filled with compassion for those who invoke you and with love for those who suffer, heavily laden with the weight of my troubles, I cast myself at your feet and humbly beg of you to take the present affair which I recommend to you under your special protection.St. Ann, please, recommend to your daughter, the Blessed Virgin Mary, and lay it before the throne of Jesus, so that He may bring it to a happy issue.St. Ann cease not to intercede for me until my request is granted. (Here ask for favor you wish to obtain.)Above all, obtain for me the grace of one day beholding my God face to face, and with You and Mary and all the saints, praising and blessing Him through all eternity. Amen.Good St. Ann, mother of her who is our life, our sweetness and our hope, pray to her for us and obtain our request. (Three times).

Saint Anne Prayer

Good St. Anne, you were especially favored by God to be the mother of the most holy Virgin Mary, the Mother of our Savior. By your power with your most pure daughter and with her divine Son, kindly obtain for us the grace and the favor we now seek. Please secure for us also forgiveness of our past sins, the strength to perform faithfully our daily duties and the help we need to persevere in the love of Jesus and Mary. Amen.

Patron Saint of: grandmothers, mothers, women in labor and house wives.

Petition for: special request, help for the deaf and blind

St. Martha

Feast Day: July 29th
Day of the Week: Tuesday
Candle Color: Green

Novena to St. Martha
(pray for 9 consecutive Tuesdays)

St. Martha, I resort to thy aid and protection. As proof of my affection and faith, I offer thee this light, which I shall burn every Tuesday. Comfort me in all my difficulties and through the great favors thou didst enjoy when the Saviour was lodged in thy house, intercede for my family, that we be provided for in our necessities. I ask of thee, St. Martha, to overcome all difficulties as thou didst overcome the dragon which thou hadst at thy feet. Amen.

Pray 1 Our Father, 1 Hail Mary, 1 Glory be

A Prayer to St. Martha

O blessed St. Martha, your faith led Jesus to proclaim, "I am the resurrection and the life"; and faith let you see beyond his humanity when you cried out, "Lord I believe that you are the Messiah, the Son of God." With firm hope you said, "I know that God will give you whatever you ask of him", and Jesus called your brother Lazarus back from the dead. With pure love for Jesus you welcomed him into your home.

Friend and servant of our Saviour, I too am "troubled about many things". *(mention your intentions)* Pray for me that I may grow in faith, hope and love, and that Jesus, who sat at your table, will hear me and grant me a place at the banquet of eternal life. Amen.

St. Clare

Feast Day: August 11th
Day of the Week: Monday
Candle Color: White

O Glorious St. Clare! God has given you the power of working miracles continually, and the favor of answering the prayers of those who invoke your assistance in misfortune, anxiety, and distress. We beseech you, obtain from Jesus through Mary His Blessed Mother, what we beg of you so fervently and hopefully, (mention your petition) if it be for the greater honor and glory of God and for the good of our souls. Amen.

NOVENA TO SAINT CLARE

Dear St. Clare, as a young girl you imitated your mother's love for the poor of your native Assisi. Inspired by the preaching of St. Francis, who sang enthusiastically of His Lord Jesus and Lady Poverty, you gave your life to Jesus at nineteen years of age, allowing St. Francis to cut off your beautiful hair and invest you with the Franciscan habit. All through your life you offered your great suffering for your Sisters, the Poor Clares, and the conversion of souls. You greatly aided St. Francis with his new order, carrying on his spirit in the Franciscans after his death. Most of all you had a deep love of Jesus in the Most Blessed Sacrament, which fueled your vocation to love and care for the poor. Please pray for me *(mention your request)* that I will seek to keep Jesus as my first love, as you did. Help me to grow in love of the Blessed Sacrament, to care for the poor, and to offer my whole life to God. Heavenly Father, thank You for the gift of St. Clare. Through her intercession, please hear and answer my prayer, in the name of Jesus Your Son. Amen.

St. Theresa

Feast Day: October 1st
Day of the Week: Wednesday
Candle Color: Yellow

O glorious Saint Therese, whom Almighty God has raised up to aid and counsel mankind, I implore your Miraculous Intercession. So powerful are you in obtaining every need of body and soul our Holy Mother Church proclaims you a "Prodigy of Miracles...the Greatest Saint of Modern Times." Now I fervently beseech you to answer my petition (mention specifics here) and to carry out your promises of spending Heaven doing good upon the earth...of letting fall from Heaven a Shower of Roses. Henceforth, dear Little Flower, I will fulfill your plea "to be made known everywhere" and I will never cease to lead others to Jesus through you. Amen.

Petition for: problems with alcoholism and drugs, spiritual growth, protection, restore faith and tuberculosis.

St. Francis of Assisi

Feast Day: October 4th
Day of the Week: Monday
Candle Color: Brown

The Peace Prayer

Lord, make me an instrument of Thy peace;Where there is hatred, let me sow love;Where there is injury, pardon;Where there is error, the truth;Where there is doubt, the faith;Where there is despair, hope;Where there is darkness, light;And where there is sadness, joy.O Divine Master,Grant that I may not so much seekTo be consoled, as to console;To be understood, as to understand;To be loved as to love.For it is in giving that we receive;It is in pardoning that we are pardoned;And it is in dying that we are born to eternal life. Amen.

Patron Saint of: Animals, birds, firemen and needle workers.

Petition for: better understanding, peace, gain spiritual wisdom and to help with problems.

St. Christopher

Feast Day: July 25th
Day of the Week: Wednesday
Candle Color: Red

Prayer for Motorists

Grant me O Lord a steady hand and watchful eye. That no one shall be hurt as I pass by Thou gavest life, I pray no act of mine may take away or mar that gift of Thine Shelter those, dear Lord, who bear me company, From the evils of fire and all calamity. Teach me to use my car for others' need; Nor miss through love of undue speed the beauty of the world; that thus I may with joy and courtesy go on my way. St. Christopher, holy patron of travellers, protect me and lead me safely to my destiny.

SAFE JOURNEY

Dear Saint Christopher protect me today in all my travels along the road's way give your warning sign if danger is near so that I may stop while the path is clear. Be at my window and direct me through when the vision blurs from out of the blue carry me safely to my destined place, like you carried Christ in your close embrace.
Amen.

Patron Saint of: bachelors, bus drivers, motorist, and travelers.

Petition for: protection from accidents, safe travel, and against storms.

Prayer to St. Matthew

Feast Day: September 21st
Day of the Week:
Candle Color:

O Glorious St. Matthew, in your Gospel you portray Jesus as the longed-for Messiah who fulfilled the Prophets of the Old Covenant and as the new Lawgiver who founded a Church of the New Covenant. Obtain for us the grace to see Jesus living in his Church and to follow his teachings in our lives on earth so that we may live forever with him in heaven.

Petition for: money and money problems

OPEN ROAD PRAYER

I invoke the sublime influence of the eternal father to obtain success in all the subjects of my life and to smooth all difficulties that are in my way. I invoke the aid of the Holy Spirit, so that my house prospers and my company and my person receive a message of good luck, sent by the divine providence. Oh great hidden power, I implore your supreme majesty so that you separate me from danger, at the precise moment, that my way is illuminated by the light of fortune. I shall receive the infinite blessing of the sky. I believe in God all powerful Father, Amen!

Padre Pio

Prayer for Healing

Beloved Padre Pio, Today I come to add my prayer to the thousands of prayers offered to thee every day by those who love and venerate thee. They ask for cures and healings, earthly and spiritual blessings, and peace for body and mind. And because of thy friendship with the Lord, He heals those thou doth ask to be healed, and forgives those thou forgiveth.

Through thy visible wounds of the Cross, which thou didst bear for fifty years, thou wert chosen in our time to glorify the crucified Jesus. Because the Cross has been replaced by other symbols, please help us to bring it back in our midst, for we acknowledge it is the only true sign of salvation. As we lovingly recall the wounds that pierced thy hands, feet and side, we not only remember the blood thou didst shed in pain, but thy smile, and the invisible halo of sweet-smelling flowers that surrounded thee, the perfume of sanctity.

In thy kindness, please help me with my own special request:

[mention here your petition, making the Sign of the Cross]

Bless me and my loved ones. In the name of the Father, the Son and the Holy Spirit. Amen.

Prayer to Saint Pio

O God, Thou didst give Saint Pio of Pietrelcina, Capuchin priest, the great privilege of participating in a unique way in the Passion of Thy Son, grant me through his intercession the grace of [name your request] which I ardently desire; and above all grant me the grace of living in conformity with the death of Jesus, to arrive at the glory of the resurrection.

Glory be to the Father . . . [three times].

Novena To The Sacred Heart Of Jesus

I. O my Jesus, You have said, 'Truly I say to you, ask and it willbe given you, seek and you will find, knock and it will beopened to you.' Behold, I knock, I seek and ask for the grace of…

Our Father… Hail Mary… Glory be to the Father…Sacred Heart of Jesus, I place all my trust in you.

II. O my Jesus, You have said, 'Truly I say to you, if you askanything of the Father in my name, He will give it to you.'Behold, in Your name, I ask the Father for the grace of…

Our Father… Hail Mary… Glory be to the Father…Sacred Heart of Jesus, I place all my trust in you.

III. O my Jesus, You have said, 'Truly I say to you, heaven andearth will pass away but my words will not pass away.'Encouraged by Your infallible words, I now ask for the grace of…

Our Father… Hail Mary… Glory be to the Father…Sacred Heart of Jesus, I place all my trust in you.

O Sacred Heart of Jesus, for whom it is impossible not to havecompassion on the afflicted, have pity on us poor sinnersand grant us the grace which we ask of You, through the Sorrowful and Immaculate heart of Mary, Your tender mother and ours.

Hail, Holy Queen… St. Joseph, foster father of Jesus, pray for us

Christmas Novena

Hail and Blessed be the hour and the moment in which the Son of God was born of the most pure Virgin in Bethlehem at midnight in piercing cold.

In that our vouchsafe, O my God, to hear my prayers and grant my desires through the merits of Jesus Christ and His Blessed Mother. Amen

It is piously believed that those who recite the above (15) times a day from the Feast of St. Andrew November 30th, until Christmas Day, will receive whatever favor they ask.

Morning Offering Prayer

O Jesus, through the Immaculate Heart of Mary, I offer you my prayers, works, joys and sufferings of this day in union with theHoly Sacrifice of the Mass throughout the world. I offer them for all the intentions of your Sacred Heart: the salvation of souls, the reparation for sin, and the reunion of all Christians. I offer them for the intentions of our bishops and of all Apostles of Prayer, and in particular for those recommended by our Holy Father this month.

Road Opener Psalms

Psalms 16:11: Thou wilt shew me the path of life: in thy presence is fullness of joy; at thy right hand there are pleasures for evermore.

Psalms 23:3: He restoreth my soul: he leadeth me in the paths of righteousness for his name's sake.

Psalms 25:4: Shew me thy ways, O Lord; teach me thy paths.

Psalms 25:10: All the paths of the LORD are mercy and truth unto such as keep his covenant and his testimonies.

Psalms 119:35: Make me to go in the path of thy commandments; for therein do I delight.

Psalms 119:105: Thy word is a lamp unto my feet, and a light unto my path.

Prayer for Peace

O Lord Jesus Christ, Who said to Your Apostles: "Peace I leave with you, My peace I give to you," regard not my sins but the faith of Your Church, and deign to give her peace and unity according to Your Will: Who live and reign, God, world without end. Amen.

A Prayer for Peace of Mind (by Saint Francis Xavier Cabrini)

FORTIFY me with the grace of Your Holy Spirit and give Your peace to my soul that I may be free from all needless anxiety, solicitude and worry. Help me to desire always that which is pleasing and acceptable to You so that Your will may be my will.

Psalm 23
King James Version

23 The Lord is my shepherd; I shall not want.

2 He maketh me to lie down in green pastures: he leadeth me beside the still waters.

3 He restoreth my soul: he leadeth me in the paths of righteousness for his name's sake.

4 Yea, though I walk through the valley of the shadow of death, I will fear no evil: for thou art with me; thy rod and thy staff they comfort me.

5 Thou preparest a table before me in the presence of mine enemies: thou anointest my head with oil; my cup runneth over.

6 Surely goodness and mercy shall follow me all the days of my life: and I will dwell in the house of the Lord for ever.

Holy Spirit Novena

Dearest Holy Spirit, confiding in Your deep, personal love for me, I am making this novena for the following request, if it be Your Holy Will to grant it: *(mention your request).*

Teach me, Divine Spirit, to know and seek my last end; grant me the holy fear of God; grant me true contrition and patience. Do not let me fall into sin. Give me an increase of faith, hope and charity, and bring forth in my soul all the virtues proper to my state in life.

Make me a faithful disciple of Jesus and an obedient child of the Church. Give me efficacious grace sufficient to keep the Commandments and to receive the Sacraments worthily. Give me the four Cardinal Virtues, Your Seven Gifts, Your Twelve Fruits. Raise me to perfection in the state of life to which You have called me and lead me through a happy death to everlasting life. I ask this through Christ our Lord, Amen.

Candles and Their Meaning

Anybody can a light a candle but if your looking for a special intention it requires a lot more than that. You have to focus no distractions, cleanse the candle (you probably bought it from a store which it there picked everyone's energy you have to remove it "cleanse"), anoint the candle, say your prayer, focus and place all your energy into that candle for your intention.

Candles can be lit for many reasons, love, health, family, protection, money, guidance, peace etc. It's your faith that makes your candle powerful. Below I have listed the colors and their meaning. This will help you choose the candle that is right for you.

Pink symbolizes love, tenderness, affection, and togetherness. Light a pink candle to bring/attract love; keep a relationship together, sweet. Sprinkle a little bit of cinnamon it as well.

Orange symbolizes happiness, enthusiasm, fun, vitality, attraction and friendship. Great to burn for success in business or new employment opportunity, and to attract new things.

Red powerful color symbolizing powerful vibrations, strength, courage, sexual attraction, positive energy. Red candles are lit for protection from enemies, evil eyes, psychic attacks, block negativity and to conquer fear.

Blue symbolizes tranquility, peace, calm, blessing, blessing in the home or business, youth and innocence. Light a blue candle for your home, business, to keep the peace, calm the nerves and mental health or help someone who is depressed.

Purple symbolizes royalty, wisdom, psychic, and dignity. Light a purple to help block black magic, protect from evil and for psychic awareness.

Yellow symbolizes, friendship and communication and creativity. Light a yellow candle open up communication lines with others, help friendships, peace, and to get in touch with your creative side.

Green symbolizes, fertility, abundance, good fortune, good luck and good health. Light a green candle to draw money, good health, promote balance and harmony in ones life.

Brown well balanced color used to gain financial success, attract money or help a financial situation. Also symbolizes family.

White symbolizes purity, truth, sincerity and spiritualty. White candles can be burned in substitute of other candles if needed. White is very powerful when used and sends off positive vibrations. Always good to have white candles available.

Black is the most controversial of all. Some people believe black candles are black magic, evil. But I believe its what your gut tells you, what your intentions are will show you how it works. Black candles absorb negativity and hen burned they release it. Its absorbs whatever intention you put into it. Is your energy good or bad.

Your Sign-Candle Color

Sign	Date of Birth	Candle Color
LEO	July 24-Aug 22	Green & Red
ARIES	March 21-April 19	White & Rose Pink
SAGITTARIUS	Nov 21-Dec 20	Green Gold & Red
TAURUS	April 20-May 19	Red & Yellow
GEMINI	May 20-June 18	Light Blue and Red
CANCER	June 19-July 23	Green and Brown
SCORPIO	Oct 22-Nov 20	Golden Brown and Black
LIBRA	Sept 22-Oct 21	Red, Black and Light blue
CAPRICORN	Dec 21- Jan 19	Deep Red, Brown, grey
PISCES	Feb 19-March 20	Pink, Green, White & Black
VIRGO	Aug 23-Sept 21	Gold and Black
AQUARIUS	Jan 20-Feb 18	Blue, Pink, and Green

Biography

Tara has lived on Staten Island all her life with her brother and family. Over the years Tara has been through many obstacles in her life. One of the hardest ones was loosing her mother to Lung Cancer in 2012. Knowing her mother would have wanted her to, Tara always kept moving forward and kept a positive attitude on life. She has helped many people along the way overcome their own obstacles as well. Tara's main goal is to make sure her client leaves happy, positive, and having the power to accomplish anything they put their mind to.

PROFESSIONAL ACCOMPLISHMENTS – Tara's clientele consists of various people from all around the world. Tara is not only about readings but counseling and helping guide those who are lost, suffering from addictions such as abusive relationships. Tara also has a 100% rating from client satisfaction thus far. It's not about the money with her, its more about helping, healing and guiding her clients. Tara's favorite guides are angels and saints, which guide her during her readings. Tara has also made her own Oracle Angel Card Deck called "Angels Cards by Tara" which she designed for anyone to use. She wanted to not only help those who seek to be more spiritual but anyone who seeks daily guidance from their angels.

SERVICES OFFERED - Tara offers oracle, tarot, medium and picture readings. She is available for private, phone and email readings, charity events and fundraisers. She also prepares, spiritual baths, candles and oils. Tara also provides private one and one sessions for spiritual and home cleansings as well as classes for spiritual guidance. Visit Tara's web page at www.psyhictara.com for more information.

BIBLIOGRAPHY

- *www.catholic.org*
- *The Magical Power of the Saints-Evocation and Candle Rituals-Reverend Ray T. Malbrough*

www.ingramcontent.com/pod-product-compliance
Lightning Source LLC
Chambersburg PA
CBHW071802040426

42446CB00012B/2668